BEFORE YOU HIT 40:

FORTY-ONE PIVITOL WISDOM NUGGETS

ISBN: 978-1-7341346-5-0

LOC Control #: 2019957910

Publisher, Editor and Book Design: Fiery Beacon Publishing House

Fiery Beacon Consulting and Publishing Group

This work was produced in Greensboro, North Carolina, United States of America.

Before You Hit 40:

Forty-One Pivotal Life Nuggets

Brandi L. Rojas

My Dedication

To God my Father, thank you for life. I am nothing without You.

To my Husband and children, your love for me is irreplaceable. I pray that God will continue to use me in ways that make you proud.

To my Mother and Brother, I know you have seen me through many places; may this book show you that it was and is all worth it.

To every supporter and friend, may the words within this book fuel, ignite and position you for greatness.

Table of Contents

The Forward

Welcome to 40, 30, 20 are whatever age you are! No matter the reason or the season of your life that you are in, I am so glad that you are here. My name is Brandi L. Rojas and I serve as the vessel by which this literary work is written. Every book that I write is especially important to me and this one holds its own special place too, as I celebrate my 41st birthday on January 3, 2020.

Now some of you may not consider this to be a "monumental birthday" and you may even be wondering why I did not release this when I turned 40. In all honestly I lost all of my notes (cue suspenseful music!) Yes me, I lost all of my notes, my keywords, that I wanted to be in this book. At the time of course I was upset, but looking back, feel that it was not by mistake but an "intentional displacement." You see, there was a lot that I needed to learn in my 40th year; this past year was necessary to equip me to bring this book to you! I have so much more to learn and so many more amazing things to experience but I could not think of a better way to celebrate this next birthday without sharing these wisdom nuggets with you.

As you read, I am praying a few things for you:

1. Be open to what you are about to read. One of the things God has called me to a ministry of transparency, so there are things I will share that I pray triggers the best in you.

2. Be willing to think and write! After something has been "triggered" I believe one of the next best things that can happen is a plan and relentless execution! Space is being provided for you to write your personal experiences and even ways that you can embark on the next level of YOU!

3. Become a Finisher! Life has a funny way of allowing us to pick something up and laying it back down and finding it years later with a look of surprise and memories of "the day you wrote" what you said you wanted. Let your reflections and the words of destiny come alive with this book!

I believe that this book has the capacity to touch everyone! Maybe you are turning 40, already did or you are not even close to this magic number; no matter WHERE you are I pray that this helps.

Nugget #1

Gratitude

The quality of being thankful; readiness to show appreciation for and to return kindness.

Whew! So you made it another day! I remember the day called forty like it was yesterday, but more than that, I remember many days I have experienced this year. I remember the first time I had to tell someone how old I was and how our youngest reacted when I told someone that I was "25 in my mind."

"NO MOM you're not 25 – you're 40! You're 40 Mom!"

Reality checks, especially from our children, bring out the truth in us, but that day I learned something very important: Never be ashamed of how old you are but instead, be grateful! It was in that though that I began to reflect on friends I went to school with who are no longer here. I reflected on how many times bondage and death

11

came for me and where I would be if it had actually worked. This reality caused gratitude to overwhelm my soul and even drove me to tears. So many times my mom often said, "Don't rush! Take your time", and moments like this causes those words to echo more loudly than ever as I now look at my own children and tell them the very same thing. When you have a teenager who has the "cannot wait until I turn 18" syndrome, you shake your head as you realize the bills and responsibility that flowed right on in with that age, too!

So as we embark on forty, you may wonder why I am giving you forty- one nuggets? Well, it is one to grow on of course! As we go forth on this ride take a moment to remember those life lessons that you heard as a youth that you did not understand then but definitely understand now! (No worries, I will not tell them that they were right; this is just between you and this book!)

My Life Nuggets

_____

_____

_____

_____

_____

_____

_____

_____

_____

_____

_____

_____

_____

_____

_____

Nugget #2

Positioning

put or arrange (someone or something) in a particular place or way.

Positioning, huh? What in the world does this have to do with my next decade of life? Well, I am so glad that you asked! Interesting fact, I have been dancing since I was three years old, and over the past twenty-four years, have been focusing on dance arts in the realm of ministry. I have taught ballet, modern, hip-hop, mime and even ballroom and have been able to use all of that to help impact the church. So let me share this story with you and maybe it will make a little more sense. Anytime that I teach a class, one of the first things we go over is called "technique," or for lack of better terms, "positioning." These positions, marked 1st-5th, are the basic positions of the feet and a major foundation in ballet. Each of these teachings are taught first, not for purposes of looking pretty, but is used to build other movements upon it and to prevent injury. Wait! Stop! Yes, you read that right - PREVENT INJURY! Now, this positioning works in multiple ways – for some reading this you may be thinking about positioning of self and for others, you may be considering the positioning of others. Please know, that neither approach is wrong so let's prepare our hearts to address both, shall we?

When I looked up the biblical meaning for the number forty, I came across these words:

"generally symbolizes a period of testing, trial or probation."[1]

Man, that does not sound too promising, but in actuality, it is a blessing! As I looked deeper, I was reminded of the journey that Moses and the Israelites took and the forty days and nights he spent in God's presence to receive the law (in other words, to become equipped and help his legacy too!) The Israelites took a journey that should have taken only eleven days and made it last forty YEARS. Maybe as you are reading these words, you are contemplating the parts of your own life that felt like you were going in circles. There is an old song that comes to mind:

---

[1] https://www.biblestudy.org/bibleref/meaning-of-numbers-in-bible/40.html

"You got me going in circles (oh round and round I go)
You got me going in circles
(oh round and round I go, I'm spun out over you)"[2]

While this song refers to a man who is head over heels in love, some of us have found ourselves "spun" over our circumstances, issues and problems. You know, we can even liken it unto the way we feel when we constantly spin in circles without finding a "spot" to keep us grounded. In dance, spotting refers to finding a unique object to focus on every time you complete a cycle in an effort to keep you focused and more likely to accomplish the desired number of rotations no matter the number of them attempted. See, positioning also brings us into the place of becoming grounded enough to complete thing or courageous enough to turn off the cycles in our lives.

One of the first things I must say I learned, was seeing the cycles for what they were. While some may have tried to blame it on the enemy (tried that) or even called it "the elephant in the room" (tried that too), we have to become un-dizzy enough to realize that we allowed it. WHEW! That seems like an early bombshell, but the moment we admit that we allowed it, we can become so much better for it.

---

[2] "Going in Circles" by The Friends of Distinction

We are not living to our highest potential - we allowed it.

People may be taking advantage of a "good situation," but we allowed it.

Procrastination has just about swallowed our New Year's confession - but we allowed it.

Maybe these examples did not come down your personal road, but I pray that it will help you to begin thinking about what the absence of proper positioning has allowed in your life. I close with this, when a person has a vision to build a building, they have certain requirements to fulfill to ensure the structure's safety and proper existence. Sometimes, we slap down foundation and begin to build what looks like what God said, only to see it crumble and wonder why. Remember this, no building can stand properly, when the foundation is faulty; it must be properly positioned, and if I may add, until the foundation is what it needs to be the rest of the project cannot be approved. This re-positioning WILL be uncomfortable and may require you releasing those you have been with for years but now, see that they were okay with seeing you live a mediocre life. You may say YES to this shift and find yourself having to even decline doing business with certain people; whatever God says just trust Him. Fix the foundation, fix it today and prepare to flourish!

My Life Nuggets

_____

_____

_____

_____

_____

_____

_____

_____

_____

_____

_____

_____

_____

_____

Nugget #3

Focus

an act of concentrating interest or activity on something; the state or quality of having or producing clear visual definition.

Lately, I have found myself saying:

"I need some new glasses!"

Many do not know, but I grew up wearing glasses. By the time I reached college, I transitioned to wearing contacts that took me from pretty brown eyes to grey and green, and you could not tell me that I was not cute, either! For me, it became more for fashion but truthfully it was a vehicle to help me FOCUS. I cannot tell you how many people in this world have purchased cars well out range because they forgot that they only needed it to get where they needed to go, not to "look cute" and found themselves paying more than they were ready for all because they lost their focus. The truth of the matter is, we have all done it whether we want to admit to it or not.

When I was in college, I learned the "power" of credit. No, I did not take a class for it and no I never had a sit-down conversation with my parents about the power of credit (that conversation came in the form of the cashier who said, "I'm sorry ma'am, this isn't going through." This was followed by a minimum payment and "Congratulations, we have increased your limit.") I was the one that would walk in a store, and because I was not a "shopper" like that, I would get a sales associate and simply say, "Hey! Can I get the whole outfit that mannequin has on?" Yes, that is how my shopping trips went for the most part. In these moments, though my mom never trained me on credit, she often warned me in her own subtle way about what I just bought and asking how I paid for it followed by questions of how I would pay it back. College should have been focused on school and establishing great credit but instead was centered around impressing many I would never see again and filling the gapping hole in my heart. I lost my focus and there was no outfit, makeup, music or otherwise that could fill it other than to regain my focus, fix what was wrong in me and prepare to recover all.

My Life Nuggets

_____

_____

_____

_____

_____

_____

_____

_____

_____

_____

_____

_____

_____

_____

_____

Nugget #4

Endurance

the fact or power of enduring an unpleasant or difficult process or situation without giving way.

"I Won't Complain"[3]

I've had some good days

I've had some hills to climb

I've had some weary days

And some lonely nights

But when I look around and I think

Things over...all of my good days,

They outweigh my weary days - I won't complain

Sometimes my clouds hang low

I can hardly see the road

I ask the question-"Lord...Why so much pain?"

But He knows what's best for me

Although my weary eyes cannot see

And I say, Thank you Lord - I won't complain...

He dries all my tears away

Turn my dark nights into days

---

[3] " I Won't Complain by Rev. Paul Jones, 1993

And I say, Thank you Lord - I won't complain...

God has been good to me
He's been so good to me
Better than you or this old world could ever be
He's been so good, He's been so good to me...
He dries all my tears away
Turn my dark nights into days
And I say, Thank you Lord...

I won't complain

This is a song that I have heard so many times and every time I see a crowd of individuals close their eyes and rock or look intently to the vessel singing and nodding their head in agreement. Growing up at New Light Missionary Baptist Church in Greensboro, North Carolina, this song regularly filled the sanctuary. At that age, I could not really comprehend how or why people found themselves in tears, especially when the song said that they would not complain. I could only think that God must have been moving on them and causing them to cry, especially on the "God has been too good to me," part. This also seems to be a song shared most often at funerals, too as people gather to celebrate the life of their loved one and attest to the fact that the one whom they celebrate, endured.

The late Dr. Myles Munroe said:

"The graveyard is the **richest place** on the surface of the earth because there you will see the books that were not published, ideas that were not harnessed, songs that were not sung, and drama pieces that were never acted."

What a heavy statement, but true. How many dreams have been forfeited and now live in the cemetery? How many visions have been assassinated all because of what someone said as they contested the very idea? For some of you, the thought that you endured is too much to handle because you have either (1) chosen to believe the "benchwarmers" or (2) have discounted the importance of what you have accomplished over the course of your life until now.

Do you realize how much you really have accomplished and even survived? Do you know that there are people who did not make It and died with their dreams tucked away because of others' opinions? Do you know that in these _____ years of life (fill in the blank), that you have survived more than what others would even fathom? Even if you are still sitting in the process of your dreams, thank God for the endurance, patience and

27

strength to continue to pursue. If you are waiting for the "go ahead" from others, let go of that cycle today and press forward into the God-ordained purpose for which God has created you! I promise you, it may not be easy, but it will be worth it!

My Life Nuggets

_____

_____

_____

_____

_____

_____

_____

_____

_____

_____

_____

_____

_____

_____

Nugget #5

Boldness

willingness to take risks and act innovatively; confidence or courage.; the quality of having a strong, vivid, or clear appearance.

Whew! I will never forget the moment when THIS baby showed up. BOLDNESS! You see, it is that part of you that rises up and says NO MORE! It is that place in you that sends the candy-coated verbiage away and tells it like it is, not in a hurtful way but in a way that helps to invoke truth, responsibility and response!

I have always been described as a cheerleader; matter of fact, many have told me that I probably should have been one at least in high school. (I was a dancer so that should be close enough, right?) There is a saying that goes a little something like this.

OLDER AND BOLDER!

What I have come to understand is that for some, older does not have to show up but experience does! I have always been one to take a lot, in other words, people had

31

the ability to do so much to me without me saying a word and the cheerleader in me would still encourage and push the "offender" without me ever telling them what they did. Needless to say, this was not easy — I have literally had to pray for people with my whole heart that I knew hated me, but being what some call an "internalist", I did not know any other way. With boldness comes TRUTH. Yes, TRUTH. The hard part about this is knowing how to share it especially when you have held it in for so long.

On the other end, there are those who are what I call "externalists"; in other words and excuse my intentional grammatical flare, they ain't holdin' nothin'!!!! (Hey, do not forget, this is my birthday book and I can be as country as I want to be!) One thing I love about God is the Husband that He blessed me with. While I have in times past been an internalist and "processor" of sorts, he is a straight shooter! Oh yes, when something goes down, he wants to handle it right then. At first I thought it was the strangest thing because in my mind, being a processor was safer since it afforded me the ability to think my thoughts through like fine wine before I share something prematurely that could literally tear a person's head off, but over time, have learned to appreciate his approach.

So as boldness shows up just remember:

1. Be strategic.

2. Be kind.

3. Be honest.

You can do this!

My Life Nuggets

_____

_____

_____

_____

_____

_____

_____

_____

_____

_____

_____

_____

_____

_____

_____

Nugget #6

Flexibility

the quality of bending easily without breaking; the ability to be easily modified.; willingness to change or compromise.

This is the message that came to Jeremiah from the LORD: 2 "Jeremiah, go down to the potter's house. I will give you my message there."

3 So I went down to the potter's house and saw him working with clay at the wheel. 4 He was making a pot from clay. But there was something wrong with the pot. So the potter used that clay to make another pot. With his hands he shaped the pot the way he wanted it to be.

Jeremiah 18:1-4

Just in case you did not read the definition, or maybe it went in one ear and out the other:

FLEXIBILITY — the quality of bending easily without breaking; the ability to be easily modified; willingness to change or compromise.

Now that we have re-established this truth, let's talk! I remember when God showed me the above scripture to minister, known to most as the potter and the clay. It seemed perfect, as I could only think about the beauty of the potter forming this clay into something beautiful; what I did not consider was the process therein. As I began researching this process (in biblical times) the first requirement was for the potter to go out and find not dirt, but clay. Understand that dirt can be hard and unable to be moved when it is dry; in the eyes of a potter this is not befitting to make a vessel because anything dry is considered to be dust and to them dust meant nothing more than death. In other words, the potter was looking for something living! The potter was looking for something that could be used to create a miraculous piece of art. When the potter went out to find what they would use, it is said that they knew what was able to qualify based on what they could step on and see their foot imprint in return. You see, by this point in life you may have had some "stepped on" moments, you know, those places where you say, "God how much more!?" I get it, I have been there.

36

I recently sat and reviewed the things I have gone through over these last ten years.

I have lost a marriage before. I have lost a dance studio before.

I have lost friends I never thought I would lose. I have felt displaced in the church.

I have found myself in places I never thought I would go.

But most of all, I have and still am, RECOVERING ALL and so will YOU!

My Life Nuggets

_____

_____

_____

_____

_____

_____

_____

_____

_____

_____

_____

_____

_____

_____

_____

_____

Nugget #7

Survival

the state or fact of continuing to live or exist, typically in spite of an accident, ordeal, or difficult circumstances.

I'm a survivor! I'm not gon' give up!
I'm not gon' stop! I'm gon' work harder!
I'm a survivor! I'm gonna make it!
I will survive! Keep on surviving! [4]

So did I catch you singing? Did I catch you reminiscing? Yes, no, maybe so! Regardless of where you are in this moment YOU SURVIVED! Yes you! Hear me loud and clear — you SURVIVED! The above definition shares a few key things with us that I want to bring out.

You have survived:

1. **In spite of an accident:** These are the things that are out of your control or that you never planned. When accidents happen, some of us have a hard time not placing blame. We feel like we should have known or done more over things that we could

---

[4] "Survivor" by Destiny's Child (2001)

have never controlled at all. It is time to be free from that!

2. **Ordeal:** This is defined as, "a horrific or painful experience, especially a protracted one." In other words, something that hurts more than we would ever want to admit and lasts longer than we would ever want to endure. The thing about this place is that it could be something that we have involved ourselves in such as abuse, cycles or bad decisions; it could also be something such as outside situations that we watch from the outside that do not involve us but we take the weight of it. Again, it is time to be free.

3. **Difficult Circumstances:** There is a scripture that says: "The spirit is willing, but the flesh is weak. (Matthew 26:41) One of the hardest places to go through can be the moments when you find out, for example, the "reason, season, lifetime" categories have been completely unbalanced and this truth can cause us to have to re-categorize or eliminate people placements altogether. One of the major ideas we have talked about in society is the process of "finding our tribe." Can I be honest? I thought I found my tribe, but I was wrong. I tried to find it

again, strike 2. I tried to re-establish it again, strike
3. Okay, I believe that you get the point now. I,
Brandi, tried to establish MY tribe instead of simply
allowing God to establish it for me. I often found
myself broken and brokenhearted, alone and
feeling abandoned when all I really had to do was
allow GOD to establish it. Let's say it one more
time, it is time to be free!

My Life Nuggets

Nugget #8

Overcome

defeat (an opponent); prevail.

One of the most beautiful things we can ever learn to do is OVERCOME. Now let me be honest, this is not easy, I repeat, this is not easy but is completely required if you want what God showed you for your life. Overcoming something usually implies that I have met up with something that has the potential to knock the wind out of me, but thanks be to God, has not. As you read this and even as you prepare to write down your own life nuggets, I encourage you to write down what you have overcome and superseded.

A few days ago, I was challenged by a friend to write down a few things, and in doing what she said I found myself looking at what I had overcome over the last ten years; this was pivotal for me being that we are about to enter another decade. You see, if my twenty-year-old Brandi had told my thirty-year-old Brandi what I was about to be processed through and that in spite of that I would

OVERCOME, there is no way that I would have believed her. Were the last ten years of my life horrible? Absolutely not as you will see shortly! As I noted the things that happened, I can say now with tears, only God kept me through those places.

In 2009, I had to drop out of school due to a nervous breakdown, lost my dance studio, marriage, home and ended up leaving the church I attended for thirteen years. I found myself becoming what I said I would never be — a single parent. Hurt, feeling abandoned and confused, I went straight to club to numb and mask my pain.

In 2010, I found myself dating the wrong man who ultimately had me involved in a place that I never imagined I would be. Still processing my hurt in what I considered the best way I knew how, I was still being asked to minister in dance at various places. I would go, impart and leave. One day after dance ministry, God simply said, "I just want to make you whole," and I, the prodigal daughter returned to Him. In late 2010, after ministering in that same place, I injured my leg; this injury, according to the doctors, was a paralysis that had no tears and no surgery available but was subject to being healed in time. Two weeks later, while crying in my apartment, God called me to preach His gospel again and I said YES. It was also during this time that I met the love of my life, who remained as my true friend through this entire process and is now my Husband.

In 2011, on February 27, I stood before God and witnesses to deliver my initial sermon entitled, "The Diamond Aftermath." It was in that same year that I launched my very first conference meeting, "Worship and Warfare."

In 2012, I received the word that it was time for me to begin the ministry ordination process. As I embraced the call, Holy Spirit impressed upon me that I could not go forward until I received the blessing from my former Pastor at my last church. I had not visited that place in years, the pain was too deep. One Thursday night, it just so "happened" that I got off work early. My plan was to go home and spend a quiet evening with my son, but God's plan was for me to get over my pain before He would elevate me to this next level in Him. I walked in and took my seat; I knew that some were looking at me like I was crazy, after all, my process was pretty public, but I had to be there. After bible study was over, I received the next instruction: write a letter of apology for how I left minus what I experienced, and simply let my first spiritual Father know that I was sorry for how I left and what God had done since that time. I never received a formal call confirming that he had received my package which included a copy of my initial sermon but could feel that he had it and that all was well. My Husband asked me to be his wife and we married on June 9, 2012. One week later at a restaurant, I ran into the First Lady who said these words:

"Bishop received your letter and cd and he said that he is so proud of you."

With tears in my eyes I knew that all was completely and totally well. A few weeks later, on June 22, 2012, I was ordained as an Elder in the Lord's church and a week later found out that my Husband and I were expecting our daughter, Sarai. In September 2012, we received the mandate to begin a bible study in our area; we named it The LiveWire. This bible study began online and took place in our home. We were happy with that, but God wanted more in 2013.

In 2013, January 27 to be exact, we were installed as Pastors and continued the mandate in our home. On March 15, 2013 we had our daughter in the presence of my

Husband, Mother, Doctors, Nurses and body bags to be filled by my daughter and I, BUT GOD.

By September we had people literally sitting on the stairs of our home during our Sunday time of worship and had no choice but to relocate to our first location, downtown Greensboro.

From 2013-2019 we continued to serve, praise, worship and build. It was during this time that we learned things in ministry that a classroom setting could have NEVER taught us. We experienced many days of tears but many victories too! We built, lost, rebuilt, lost, gained members, lost them and rebuilt again. On April 15, 2018, our city experienced a tornado that destroyed a good portion of the Northeast side of Greensboro, North Carolina. Our upgraded space by this point, connected to two other businesses was considered to be "Ground Zero" because of the level of damage done, but after the smoke cleared the only portion left standing was our sanctuary. Despite this fact, we still had to move due to the instability of the location. This experience led us to having church in the community room of a fire house, to sharing a space with another ministry until the death of their Pastor in 2018, to now, the YWCA. We are still pressing, believing and trusting God for every portion of what He showed us.

47

So even as I have outlined here all that I have experienced, take this time to write down what you have overcome! I know that it has not always been easy BUT YOU HAVE OVERCOME!

My Life Nuggets

_____

_____

_____

_____

_____

_____

_____

_____

_____

_____

_____

_____

_____

_____

_____

Nugget #9

Visionary

(especially of a person) thinking about or planning the future with imagination or wisdom.;

relating to or able to see visions in a dream or trance, or as a supernatural apparition.

Have you ever had a vision for something great that you simply cannot shake? Ok, now before I continue, I did not mean to make that rhyme, but since we are here I am open to a record deal (this is your cue to smile)! I cannot count how many times I have had a vision over and over again or had a prophetic voice tell me something I heard years ago that continued come up. In all honesty, it felt like torture! With vision comes so many things – confidence, excitement, preparation and yes, even fear. I know you were not expecting that last one, but I had to say it and will say it again, FEAR shows up for the VISIONARY. In the book of Joshua, we find a man who is roughly eighty years old being told constantly by God and eventually by the Israelites he led, "be strong and courageous!" Now, keep in mind this man spent many years training before he was able to step into the mantle he had been training for, but he still had to be reminded to be courageous!

I will never forget the day that I closed my studio. I will not dive all the way into that experience, since that is for another book (shameless plug), but what I remember the most was how I received the most dreams, visions and prophetic words about it after I closed it. In that moment, it did not make sense and I even became upset with God and even the mouthpieces that were speaking because I could not fathom how God would allow me to have my dreams in my hand and rip it away so publicly. I could not comprehend how God would allow people to privately make bets on my failure and laugh in my face while I cried uncontrollably. That was a place, an experience, where I did not want to be – a visionary.

Has my heart been broken since then? Yes.

Have there been other moments where I said, "God why have You given me this? Yes.

Have there been places where I simply wanted to say, "I can't"? Yes.

BUT GOD! His plan is perfect, and nothing will ever be wasted. So, whatever the vision or dream take this next page to write it down fearlessly and position yourself to pursue it relentlessly.

My Life Nuggets

_____

_____

_____

_____

_____

_____

_____

_____

_____

_____

_____

_____

_____

_____

Nugget #10

Strength

the quality or state of being physically strong; the influence or power possessed by a person, organization, or country.

If you are following this book page by page, you have already found that among other things, you are one tough cookie! You have fought, cried, bled and won! In the process of the outcome of victory, it is quite possible that you got to the end of the war and like Tye Tribbett, called it a "bloody win." This is the perfect moment to be honest - the win was not of your own ability or effort, but completely happened because of the One who has empowered you to win.

In our society today, many people have adopted a practice of refusing to ask for help. I am reminded of what happens in the gym when a person is about to lift weights and as a precaution, requests the help of a spotter. This "spotter" is the one who monitors the successful lifting and maintenance of the lifter, in other words, they help to assure that the lifter has enough STRENGTH to lift what has been placed before them. In the event that it becomes too heavy or becomes more than what this champion can bare, the spotter comes in, not to eliminate the weight but to offer the added support needed to live beyond the weight. In the word of God, we find Moses who, though he had direct encounters with God, needed Aaron and Hur to lift his arms to ensure that he would win the battle before him. (Exodus 17:12-14). If we push a little bit further, we find that Hebrews 12:1-2 delivers the following encouragement and wisdom to us:

Therefore, since we are surrounded by so great a cloud of [a]witnesses [who by faith have testified to the truth of God's absolute faithfulness], stripping off every unnecessary weight and the sin which so easily *and* cleverly entangles us, let us run with endurance *and* active persistence the race that is set before us, 2 [looking away from all that will distract us and] focusing our eyes on Jesus, who is the Author and Perfecter of faith [the first incentive for our belief and the One who brings our faith to maturity], who for the joy [of accomplishing the goal] set before Him endured the cross, [b]disregarding the shame, and sat down at the right hand of the throne of God [revealing His deity, His authority, and the completion of His work].

Simply put, our strength is not our own God has the capacity to send every kind of support that we could ever need. There are people you have never met, sometimes those even know as the "I never like or comment on your posts but I'm lifting you up", people who are impacted by your strength displayed. Some will admire and receive your mentorship from afar, and if they do, no worries. Just remember to discern between the receivers and the spotters in your life, for spotters can never advise from the locker room, but instead help to lift you on the open floor.

My Life Nuggets

_____

_____

_____

_____

_____

_____

_____

_____

_____

_____

_____

_____

_____

_____

Nugget #11

Wisdom

the soundness of an action or decision with regard to the application of experience, knowledge, and good judgment.

"I will forgive you, but I will never forget what you did." Herein lies a common and misappropriated action that we have resolved to call WISDOM. You see, the older we get, the more we become less tolerant of foolishness and more cautious too. If we are not careful, we can find ourselves in a place where even those around us who are innocent can begin to look guilty. Maybe you used the following statement as a form of protection, but in the words of Dr. Juanita Bynum, "there is a difference between isolation and incubation" – let's explore this a little deeper.

When we look at isolation, we find it to be a dark place; it is coined as a necessary place that is not done by others but instead is activated by self. When one is hurt, isolation can easily be the place that they were backed into and rarely becomes the place that they simply chose to go. Incubation, on the other end is a lot like wisdom. How?

Well, let's think about it for a moment. When a baby or even an adult is placed in incubation or quarantine, it usually takes place as a result of one who is either underdeveloped or susceptible to infection should they be exposed to the "normal environment." Because of this determination, this usually requires:

1. Any visitors to be infection and illness free.

2. Special clothing for anyone that enters the room, staff or visitors.

3. Touch is restricted to those who are properly suited up and have had permission granted.

4. The food that is consumed must be carefully monitored and strategically administered.

These are just a few influencers, but know this, this determination was solidified through the practice of wisdom. In both cases, isolation and incubation, someone is hurt, however the way the "affliction" is handled can literally make all of the difference. As you read this, consider the following: In what areas do you need to adopt and utilize a new level of wisdom? Is it in your relationships, finances, thought patterns? This question may not be the most comfortable to consider but I promise you, it will bless your life. Are you ready? Ok, let's take a deep breath. Go.

My Life Nuggets

Nugget #12

Might

expressing purpose.

I might go.

I might believe.

I might win.

I might live.

All powerful expressions used the wrong way. MIGHT is not a place of indecision as we have adopted and even defined but as stated above is a platform on which we EXPRESS purpose. Maybe we should say it this way - MIGHT is how we move IN it and NOT how we think about it!

I am feeling somewhat like the famous line in the movie Malcolm X:
"Oh, I say, and I say it again, ya been had! Ya been took! Ya been **hoodwinked!**"

For years we have used "MIGHT" as a comfort, or should I say, as a blanket! We have looked and said to ourselves that MIGHT does not require action but instead gives us a pass just in case we decide to underperform or not perform at all. I dare you, no, triple dog dare you, to think about the times that you used "might" to comfortably get you out of something you knew you had no intention of doing. As I ask you, I promise, I am writing down my list too. Now here is the follow up: What if what you decided to say "might" to, had a direct link to the destiny God called you to? O wow, this conversation is getting a little tight, but as we often say, "it's right!"

It is moments like this that I am grateful that God restores time and gives us chance after chance. Now please do not take this as a moment to figure out how many more "might" conversations you can have, but instead, make a decision TODAY that you, my friend will turn "might" into MIGHT! I had a dear friend and mentee pass unexpectedly almost two years ago. Her name was Quashima and she was a fighter! She was a minstrel! She was determined. Not only were we friends but we were also partnering in business. No matter what she was going through, even if she was in the hospital, she was always pushing through. We spoke just about every day, and every conversation started with, "Aight Pastor! What we 'bout ta' takeover today," and ended with "Let's get it!" So, I submit to you right now, let's not wait anymore! Let's stop holding destiny hostage with our "might" thinking! Let's go ahead, RIGHT NOW and step into MIGHT!

You can do this – I know you can!

My Life Nuggets

_____

_____

_____

_____

_____

_____

_____

_____

_____

_____

_____

_____

_____

_____

Nugget #13

Submission

the action or fact of accepting or yielding to a superior force or to the will or authority of another person.

Why is it that people cringe during the part of the ceremony where it says, "SUBMIT?" Even as I type I already see a number of people rolling heads and eyes only to find this word still sitting here when they are done. SUBMISSION – the will of surrendering to a superior force or will of another person. While our face gets all twisted up over the thought of submitting to a spouse or even church (yes I said it), we dare not consider the other things that we willfully submit to without argument (most of the time.)

When your job gives you the schedule and break time - we submit.

When a price is stated for a given good or service, most of the time, we submit.

When God has given us a Word, but our mind wants to tell us otherwise, sometimes, we submit.

I have come to find out that it is not hard to submit when you have confidence in what you are submitting to. As a member of the clergy, I have actually had people ask me if we can take the "submission part" out of their vows because they just cannot imagine having to relinquish their rights or will to the love of their life for the rest of their life. Yes, I said that too, so let that sink in for a moment. Many of us have no problem to submitting to poverty, depression, anxiety, disease and the list goes on but will not surrender our will to God who reigns as the Author and Finisher of our lives. He is the one who has covered, protected, let's back up, CREATED us. He gives us new mercy and even the breath you are inhaling or exhaling right now, yet there remains a fight to surrender. What am I saying? Let us not be so quick to surrender to those things that will kill us and forsake those things that purpose to give us life, purpose and help to complete destiny. If your Husband or Wife is your GOD-ordained mate, I challenge you to examine anything in you that makes it hard for you to submit. Whether it be how you were raised, your insecurities, doubts or fears, be real enough with you to admit it so that you can fully recover from it.

My Life Nuggets

_____

_____

_____

_____

_____

_____

_____

_____

_____

_____

_____

_____

_____

_____

Nugget #14

Service

the action of helping or doing work for someone.

There is nothing like the joy of service. Every year, we hear the bells ringing outside of area businesses attached to red buckets for the sake of others. It has been said that the highest season of giving happens between November and December, the holidays. This is also the highest-rated time for people having a heart to give back, therefore bombarding people in need for a period of two months with ten months left to figure out.

For our church, one of the most beautiful things we have had the ability to do is serve, who we call, our transitional community. Society calls them "homeless," but we stand on the belief that where they are is simply a place of transition, and that a day is coming where they will be on the other side of the place of hardship. We have witnessed testimonies of those who had doctor's appointments where they were required to eat before coming but encountered the problem of having no food to eat; this was literally a

71

day where we came through on our normal route to serve sandwich bags during the day. We have also had the honor of witnessing people who were in transition last year, come in our presence with keys to their new home this year — what an amazing thing! As a church we have had the pleasure of serving countless people because of our heart of service. You see, service does not have to always be planned or be huge, for when we serve from the heart, that is all God wants from us. Your service could be your smile, your laugh or an encouraging word. You may run across a person that cannot even compose the words of where they are, but the warmth of your presence causes them to embrace hope. Maybe, your act of SERVICE could be just asking someone you know or do not know, "how can I help you today?" I know it sounds corporate to ask that but remember, there are some people who are never asked how they can **BE** served, but instead are only asked how much can be extracted from them.

Never forget to serve! This place is not fueled by the calendar but is always fueled by the heart!

My Life Nuggets

Nugget #15

Worship

honor given to someone in recognition of their merit.

I choose to worship.

I just can't give up.

I choose to worship.

My mind is made up.

He's healing me I'm going to worship. [5]

I heard this song in the summer of 2010. Having just come back to God and being reignited for Him again, I wanted nothing more than to be able to dance in this place of revival. The words of the song and the passion of the psalmist fueled my soul, confirming that I simply had to go to this new place of WORSHIP! Days of practice went forth to ensure the excellence of what we planned to offer unto God in the weeks to come.

---

[5] " I Choose to Worship," Wes Morgan, 2010.

That Sunday morning came, and like a kid on Christmas morning, I was grinning from ear to ear, anticipating the place that God was about to take us all to. We prayed and covered everything we knew to cover, entrusting all we were to Him and that His glory would be seen. The song began, and the other dance vessels and I went forth. About halfway through, while executing a kick I had done one million times before, I felt a loud "pop" followed by extreme pain and later, the feeling of fire rolling up my leg. I had been dancing for years, and had never experienced a major injury, but if I knew nothing else, I knew that this was not anything close to what we planned. The other dancers looked at me in complete confusion, and all I could do was lift my hands and give the motion for them to continue. As I laid on my back, with the pain becoming worse by the second, I could only lift my hands from where I laid and begin to worship God- it was literally all I knew to do. In that moment, I did not know how badly I was injured or even how I would get myself up once the song was over. I did not know how many people were looking at me or how I would even try to recover; all I knew to do was worship God.

At the conclusion of the song that is when the reality of what happened got real, as I found myself unable to get myself up and had to ask for help. The moment I tried to apply weight, I was not sure if was going to scream or throw up, but I knew something was wrong. They pretty much carried me to an office where I sat and wept. I could not even pull up my lyrical skirt to look at my leg because I was too afraid. As a single parent I found myself even more concerned about what the repercussions would be at work, how I would care for my son and more immediately, how I would be able to drive myself home from thirty minutes away. From that moment, to the long journey to my car, to the longer journey to my home all I could do was cry and worship.

I share this because I remember how broken I felt. Some years ago, I shared this Word:

"If God can trust you with the valley He can trust   you with the mountain (victory.)"

In the moment of the injury I thought that was the "valley," but the true "valley" was when the doctor said, "partial paralysis." For me the "valley" was when he said:

"If I were you, I wouldn't even try to dance anymore."

How do you tell someone who has been dancing for over twenty-five years at this point that this "place" may as well be where you surrender part of your purpose? I wish I could describe it properly, but in that moment once I got home, all I could do was worship and remind God of my vow to Him.

"God I told you, either I dance, or I die and it's not time for me to die, so I wait for Your healing."

Yes, I said it just like that. I knew what God promised me and I refused to allow anything less. God had done too much, said too much, promised too much and I was determined to have it even if I had to worship God through tears.

My Life Nuggets

_____

_____

_____

_____

_____

_____

_____

_____

_____

_____

_____

_____

_____

_____

_____

Nugget #16

Praise

express warm approval or admiration of.

Now, now, now, before you cue the praise break, take a deep breath! I need you to take a moment to think. Matter of fact, this may be a good place to take a lap or give God a shout because YOU MADE IT THIS FAR!!!! You have thirty seconds- GO!

One of the most rewarding things that we can embrace is the sound of praise. If we decide to be honest, we will freely admit that some of us have succeeded or fallen off the strength of who praised us. Some of us majored in different subjects, purchased vehicles and even bought cars off the thought of the praise we would receive. We have literally gotten in debt in an attempt to achieve praise, but today, I want us to really think about the praise we extend to God - it is the reason for which we exist anyway!

I cannot tell you how many times I have been in places of worship and witnessed the depths we have had to go, just to give praise to God. Whatever you do, refuse to use this to be your reason why you may not decide to go. Please understand, there have been days that I did not feel the "unction" so to speak, but I knew that where I was never changed where God is. He said in His Word that we were created to worship Him, so therefore, I have to! You see, we go in debt looking for praise, but God gave the ultimate price just for us! I mean, He literally gave the ultimate price, and all He wants from us is praise, worship and completed purpose? He never has to ask the ocean to praise Him- it just does it. He never has to say, "tree, will you praise me," but instead it just happens. He has created us all to praise Him and when we do, not only does He receive due glory, but we receive what He has stored up for us.

The cliché' statement "when praises go up, blessings come down," though it is not in the bible (I just messed up someone's theology with that one), the word itself holds true! Take Joshua for instance: they walked around the wall in silence for six days but on day seven their shout, or should I say PRAISE, brought the wall down and gave them ACCESS to what God said they could have. So, let's stop and be real right here:

What wall do you need to come down right now?

Are you willing to praise God for it right now?

Are you prepared to see the miracle on the other side right now?

Well good- let's release a praise!

My Life Nuggets

_____

_____

_____

_____

_____

_____

_____

_____

_____

_____

_____

_____

_____

Nugget #17

Legacy

a thing handed down by a predecessor; an amount of money or property left to someone in a will.

The reality of LEGACY has always been a big thing with me, even before I had kids. I ran into someone I went to college with and she said,

"Give me your business card; I know you have one because you always have."

Since college, I have always been a dreamer and pretty much unafraid to start a business, or two or eight! I have never been that person that sees an opportunity and thought it could not happen for me, but instead, simply wanted to know where to sign and where I needed to send my money to. I have always been one who has a heart for others who desire to bless their children's children and beyond, and a willing participant to help in any way that I can. It was not until I turned forty that I realized that I was using all of my push to ensure the legacy of others while watching my own seemingly fall apart; this is how it happened:

When I first started in this amazing publishing world, I was one that did not have a rate but instead simply said, "Ask God and pay me that." This practice often left me tired and heartbroken if I can be honest, because that type of pay rate is often filled with thousands of dollars' worth of work with only a $20 faith seed to show for it. This becomes even harder when you know that they would potentially pay someone else the thousands of dollars that you should have quoted. I will never forget the day that I had to tell my husband that the book I published had done well and that I was not being paid a dime to do it. See at this time, he was working upwards of eighty hours per week, which means that there were days where I saw him go to bed and wake up both from the same place I sit as I share this story with you. His look of confusion was understandable and heartbreaking as I considered how much time I took from my home, my husband and children with nothing to show for it except this "news." We were both under the impression that the project would at least provide gas for our cars, more seed for ministry or maybe a normal and well-deserved night with our children but that was not the outcome and that reality of telling my kids no again, crushed my heart.

One would think that was all it would take to make me put my big girl business hat on, but it did not. I found myself again in the same place, because my heart wanted to help everyone even if it meant paying out of my own pocket and expending irreplaceable time that I felt I would never possess again. One's love for LEGACY has the potential to be driven by the heart strings, but I have had to learn discernment and wisdom even in this. Even when I want to give everything away, I seek the release of The Father first — I have to as I work to build this legacy that God has entrusted me with. I can look around my house now and see traces of my family members who have passed — my father's table, my grandmother's crock pot, my uncle's mirror, but my push flows even deeper than that.

God has a legacy just for you — **GO FORTH.**

My Life Nuggets

_____

_____

_____

_____

_____

_____

_____

_____

_____

_____

_____

_____

_____

_____

Nugget #18

Mantles

an important role or responsibility that passes from one person to another.

Is it just me or have you found yourself in a place of asking, "God why me", too? In all seriousness, I really felt like God calling me was a joke; I did not have any living blood-related relatives to guide me through this call to ministry like many others I have seen. One thing I knew for sure was that it was something that would not allow me to sleep through it, ignore it, even through my worst places.

MANTLES come in some of the hardest places. When I was twenty-one years old, I was praying one day and I felt the pull to find my grandfather, Nehemiah Troxler. I know that sounds like it should have been a natural desire, but not so much when it is someone that you have only been able to meet one time (and that was at my Daddy's funeral). So, long story short, I found him and when I did he was on his death bed. His brother, my great-uncle Gad, answered and after confirming who I was, with total shock and disbelief, my grandfather took his last breath and died. That moment was beyond confusing because I could not help but wonder why God would be so cruel as to have me witness something like that over the phone. Nevertheless, let's press forward into this story, shall we.

It had to be around 2010 when I met my Aunt Angela, who is my father's half-sister. I was with my mom at the funeral of one of my relatives on my father's side of the family, and while greeting them at the car, saw a beautiful lady say to me with tears in her eyes, "Oh my God! Brandi!" I did not realize who she was in that moment (my mom clarified a few moments later) but when she told me I immediately began holding back tears as I took in the reality of the moment. My Aunt Angie invited me into the limo to spend a few moments with her. She kept crying and I kept sitting in disbelief. It was then that she said, "I have not felt so close to your father as I do right now since he passed. If he were here right now I just know he would tell you to keep dancing. He would tell you that he is so very proud of you!" At this point I could no longer contain myself or control my tears, as I had spent years praying that God would let my Daddy see a glimpse of what He was doing in my life. The thing that hit me the hardest was the fact that I had just met my aunt and had just closed my dance studio the year before and she did not even know that I was a dancer. It was on that day that I knew I had to stay connected to her.

During the progression of our conversations, she would tell me stories of my father and my grandfather, too. The more I spoke to her, the more understanding God released to me. As I was preparing for my ordination class, I was able to share that with her as well. With excitement, she began to talk about my grandfather, telling me that he was an Elder, a singer and the list went on. With tears in my eyes, it finally began to make sense – the phone call in the last moment of my grandfather's life, the depth of worship unto God that often erupted out of my soul and even the moments as a single mom, buying grape juice, toasting bread and having communion with my son on a regular basis. It all began to come full circle, but there was one statement she made that blessed me in a way I cannot explain, and that was when she said, "When my father, your grandfather died, I thought that the anointing on his life was buried with him but it wasn't, it's with you." The tears that flooded my eyes and even the ones I hold back even as I type in this moment are simply indescribable. I never asked for this but instead ran from it. I never wanted to preach – I was happy just to praise God through the dimensions of dance that He equipped me to execute, but

91

His plan was, and even now is so much bigger than what my mind can even begin to comprehend or contain.

So with all of this being said, there is a mantle concerning your life too.

Now is your time to say YES, to the call, purpose and mantle that has been ever so patiently waiting on you.

He is waiting for you.

My Life Nuggets

94

Nugget #19

Relationship

the way in which two or more concepts, objects, or people are connected, or the state of being connected.

Let's talk RELATIONSHIP! As a little girl, I was always the one that wanted to be friends with everybody! I remember as a child, I had a classmate that really liked a wallet my mom had just purchased for me, so I gave it to them, and boy did I get in trouble! I was the one that desired to be in relationship with even those I knew could not stand me, justified or otherwise and this characteristic followed me right into adulthood.

It has been said that there are three types of relationships that go by the names reason, season and lifetime. I can be honest and say that I have been one to mis-categorize people, but I remain determined to ask and allow God to take over this place in my life, too. There are some that I thought were just there for a reason, but their assignment was for a season. I have been the one who tagged people as lifetime, when the extent of their existence was only for a reason. I will say this, places like

95

this can be beneficial but they can hurt, too. For some, God revealed their presence in my life but for others He simply allowed them to fade to black. Now that we are "adulting" we no longer call it relationship, but instead call it our "tribe" but have you ever really considered who qualifies to be in your tribe? I know that many of us say something like, "time will prove who they are", but as we continue to live this life the truth becomes clear, that we do not have time for hits and misses. Intentional should be the path we strive for – that approach that causes us to ask the hard questions and allow God to show us the truth that surrounds us. Today is a great day to start, so take a few moments and write down your qualifications! What requirements do you have for people to be in relationship with you? Are they fair? Are you willing to provide the same?

My Life Nuggets

Nugget #20

Procrastination

the action of delaying or postponing something.

This may be a hard one, but I promise you we are going to make It through this. How many times has the enemy taken the wrap for PROCRASTINATION? How many times has a prayer that you really have not prayed, ended up becoming that alibi for what you have put off on purpose? This thing called procrastination comes with so much but if I may, allow me to pose the question that came to me when I tried to justify why it was okay to not write the next book that God had already planted in my soul:

"Who is on the brink of death all because you won't move?"

Please know, it was not a friend that asked me this but a question that erupted in my mind, as I tried to justify my place of comfort. I had given every excuse I could think of for why I was "good" with what I had already done and why nothing more should be required of me. In my eyes, it was enough that God had called me ministry, but then He

99

took it a step further and required transparent ministry of me. This requirement meant that I would often have to dig into some places that would make me cry but save other people. Many times, I would have an idea and get it written down, but the possible idea of success would drive me from it. Now I know that makes no sense, but it is where I was, especially when I had no blueprint to follow. What I was writing down was big, even huge and I had no idea how to do it or how it would work but I was willing to at least write it down. So, there I sat, with idea upon idea and journal upon journal full of notes and ideas that had not manifested, some because I would not move. No, this was not the enemy's fault and yes, I had already used the excuse of seeking God when I knew I was moving in fear and lacking faith.

I stayed in this place until one day during prayer when these words escaped my mouth like hot coals:

"God has too much going on! He does not have time to lie to you!"

I realized then, that I did not believe Him – I did not believe God. The same God I loved, worshiped honored was the same one I doubted and put in the box of my own limitations. Has procrastination caused you to put God in a box? If so, I encourage you to take Him out of that box right now! There is so much He desires to accomplish through you, but He cannot do it without your cooperation and your belief.

My Life Nuggets

_____

_____

_____

_____

_____

_____

_____

_____

_____

_____

_____

_____

_____

_____

Nugget #21

Sniper

a person who shoots from a hiding place, especially accurately and at long range.

In 2019, I decided to do something I had never done before, shoot a gun! Hold up, do not get the Wild West in your mind because it was not that type of party, but it was cool to shoot in a gun range. The first time I went was for Mother's Day, after being convinced to go by a member of our church named Brandon. He kept saying, "Pastor, you just have to go!" Now keep in mind, I know others who carry, and trust and believe I was looking at them like we were in "Set it Off!" So, on Mother's Day I rolled up in there, shaking in my boots but looking like I was ready for my newly adopted SNIPER life! Now, the range is one my favorite places to be.

If there is one thing life has taught me, it has been to fight and to attack the enemy from hidden places. Listen, for far too long we have allowed the enemy to run loose through our communities, families and the list goes on!

Instead of becoming a student on how to use our spiritual weapons, we have held the gun, took out the bullets and threw them! Now, how crazy does that look? Do you really believe that a bullet is more powerful outside of the apparatus it has been designed for? Not at all but its what some of us have done!

You see, I did not realize how good I could be in the area of shooting until that day. When I got there, they had me watch a video, sign a waiver and take a short five-minute tutorial on how to use the gun I would be using that day. At first grip, I could not believe that I was holding a gun, but I knew that if I was going to shoot that day I would have to get over it and quick! They gave me special glasses and a noise-canceling headset, but most of all, a target sheet. When I shot the first time I missed, but in that moment I was just happy that I shot the gun and did not freak out! I shot again and missed but when I began to think about the things that had come for me, I shot the target right in the head! Yes, I sure did! The more I thought, the more I did not miss but when I was afraid or distracted, I missed.

Right here and right now, I do not want you to think back with the intent on being stuck there, but instead, I want you to think back and use it as fuel to load your spiritual gun and take the enemy out! I want you to think about how many times he came for your family, health and wealth – take him out!! I need you to consider how many times he came against you with depression - take him out! I want you to consider all of what the last decade tried to do to you, realize what it did for you instead, and take the enemy out!

Let's go SNIPER! Let's go!

My Life Nuggets

_____

_____

_____

_____

_____

_____

_____

_____

_____

_____

_____

_____

_____

_____

Nugget #22

Caves

a large underground chamber, typically of natural origin, in a hillside or cliff.

I will tell you the truth, in my life, I have been good for hiding in a CAVES! Okay, so maybe not the physical caves, because that is not my type of thing, but caves within myself. Some may say that it is because of hurt or pain, and sometimes it was, but other times it was simply because of where God was processing me out of. I will be honest, many times it felt horrible; I felt as if I was losing my mind in the process, but I knew that I had to stay there. There have been moments where I have wanted to reach out, but I could not – this was a work that only God could complete and involving anyone else would have contaminated His place and His work.

Though it was not in reference to a cave, this scripture comes to mind:

The LORD is my Shepherd [to feed, to guide and to shield me],

107

I shall not want.

2 He lets me lie down in green pastures;

He leads me beside the still *and* quiet waters.

3 He refreshes *and* restores my soul (life);

He leads me in the paths of righteousness

for His name's sake.

4 Even though I walk through the [sunless] [a]valley of the

shadow of death,

I fear no evil, for You are with me;

Your rod [to protect] and Your staff [to guide], they

comfort *and* console me.

5 You prepare a table before me in the presence of my

enemies.

You have anointed *and* refreshed my head with [b]oil;

My cup overflows.

6 Surely goodness and mercy *and* unfailing love shall follow

me all the days of my life,

And I shall dwell forever [throughout all my days] in the

house *and* in the presence of the LORD.

-Psalm 23

I wish that I could say that this place is an easy one,
but it is not. Whether it be called a cave, pit or valley, I
need you to know that God is there. I need you to
understand that God uses everything, even our lowest

places, to make the most amazing stories. I never thought
that He could use depression to make something beautiful,
but He has. I did not think that He would take a church-hurt
club girl and turn her into a teaching a preaching
powerhouse vessel for His glory, but He has! He is using
everything I have endured and is causing it to be a
testimony that helps others to come out of their caves
through His still voice.

**You will not die in this place – you shall live and declare
His perfected work!**

My Life Nuggets

_____

_____

_____

_____

_____

_____

_____

_____

_____

_____

_____

_____

_____

_____

_____

Nugget #23

Failure

lack of success; the omission of expected or required action.

For every sports season, there are always two types of teams, the winners and the losers. Both teams, if they really want to win, have both spent time and money practicing and preparing for their winning moment. They have stayed up late, been forced to sit in bathtubs full of ice water and even had to nurse wounds back to health. Even these few glimpses of their life should be reason enough to win every time without fail, but they also know that FAILURE is a possibility too. The chance of this happening oftentimes becomes fuel to help them fight for the win.

Society says that there is only a 5% chance that a person will achieve a goal they write down, but they also say that one is five to ten times more likely to achieve their goal if they write it. Now I already know this sounds twisted, so let me add this to the mix: There is nothing like the pain of failure but there is nothing like the feeling of recovery after failure either. I wish I could say that I have never failed, but I cannot say that. I have failed in areas of possession and relationship too, but I am beyond grateful for the full recovery of God, even when I did not deserve it. You know, had it not been for failure many of us would not know the strength that we possess. Had it not been for failure what kind of testimony would we have and even more, how would we ever be equipped to bring anyone else through their tough places?

So let's take a moment to think like our favorite teams do, and this is something that happens whether they win or lose:

THEY REVIEW THE TAPE!

Yes, they review the tape! If they experienced a loss, they watch the tape with a goal of discovering where they went wrong. No one would want to view their own tape of failure, but at the same time, no one wants to lose again either. For the winner, they watch the "tape" with excitement as they reflect on the highs of each play and how they possessed the win but then the Coach comes in to remind them that though they won they could have still done better. In other words, the Coach still demands MORE. The Coach, God, still demands more. For me, it reminds me of something I say to my business team often:

"Don't get caught up in the confetti."

Even when you have done well, it is still worth it, wisdom
even, to review the tape of your life, find out how you could
have done it better and then - DO IT BETTER. Failure does
not have to have the last say.

My Life Nuggets

Nugget #24

Renew

give fresh life or strength to; extend for a further period the validity of (a license, subscription, or contract).

Two words, "muscle memorization"; it the "thing that causes you to do the electric slide, wobble or your favorite line dance without missing a beat. Now that we have established that, it is only fair that we use this as we uncover the word, RENEW.

It is easy to live life in autopilot. We get up, shower, get dressed, brush our teeth, get out and about, come home, eat, watch television, go to bed and do it all over again. For those of you who have massive amounts of responsibility on your plate, I know from experience that you feel the weight of the day more than others but nevertheless, you continue to press through. The truth is, life can move so very fast, so fast in fact that you find yourself needing a renewal but cannot even find the time to allow renewal to have its perfect work in your life.

In 2018, it was stated that Americans forfeited 768 million vacation days; this equates to 768 million memories and days of renewal that were not used, primarily because of two things, money and time. Maybe you are among those who do not know what renewal even looks like, but know this, renewal is for the depleted, so if that describes where you are then you are on the right page. One thing we cannot do, is to allow the responsibility of life to keep us out of balance. As a pastor I can completely relate, as it was about six years before my family and I took a vacation, and that was not even on the weekend! We found ourselves on autopilot, weary from ministry, tired of the hits we were taking yet still determined to press through. As you continue to read and prepare to write, I encourage you to use this space and write down the things that make you happy! Make a note of those things that bring you joy and peace and then begin to make a commitment to yourself that you will work to ensure that you do not miss these moments, whether it be for a few hours, a day or even a week. You deserve it!

My Life Nuggets

_____

_____

_____

_____

_____

_____

_____

_____

_____

_____

_____

_____

_____

_____

Nugget #25

Peace

freedom from disturbance; tranquility.

Peace, sweet peace – there is nothing like it. Life can sometimes make peace hard to find, but it is here, there and everywhere. For some, it is in the still and quiet moments before the whole house gets up to start their day. For others, it is in the car on your lunch break where you have those few moments to sing, cry, shout, scream or even sleep. Maybe it is in the bathroom as you prepare for your day – peace is truly everywhere you seek it.

For my last two birthdays, my husband has taken me to this beach and every single visit has been a blessing to my life, simply because of the peace I find there. I find very few things better than being able to sit on the balcony and have the sun and waves greet me in the morning. Today is my birthday, and can I say, I am in such a place of peace. I woke up this morning to my husband covering my eyes and leading me to the balcony. He told me, that when I opened my eyes I would need to look down, so I did and saw a huge message in the sand that simply said, "Happy

Bday!" I could not cry (that is a miracle), but instead stood in amazement, as my husband told me that he had nothing to do with what was written in the sand. Because I am a visionary, I closed my eyes and simply took in what God showed me:

His huge hands drawing a birthday greeting in the sand just for me.

I still have not had a weeping moment since He showed me that, but instead peace just continues to overwhelm my very soul. After forty-one years of life, I can say — I thank God for peace, for real peace.

⁷ And the peace of God [that peace which reassures the heart, that peace] which transcends all understanding, [that peace which] stands guard over your hearts and your minds in Christ Jesus [is yours].

Philippians 4:7

Receive His peace as your own today.

My Life Nuggets

_____

_____

_____

_____

_____

_____

_____

_____

_____

_____

_____

_____

_____

Nugget #26

Midwife

a person or thing that helps to bring something into being or assists its development.

Push, baby, push! What a way to start a nugget but here we are! Now is your time to push! Though this sounds like this should be the conclusion, it is here, maybe for that one person reading who feels like you lost your "baby", your dream or vision; it is not lost, but simply waiting for you to push.

In Exodus we find two midwives who are charged by the king to ensure the death of every male Israelite newborn. Long story short, they refuse and as a result, are blessed. I once said that I was tired of feeling like I was the one who would help everyone else deliver in sterile and purposed places, while I delivered in dark and unsanitary alleys. Though this was my thoughts, I know that I am not alone. Many of us have prayed for others, oftentimes the same things we desired, and watched it manifest for them while we still waited. This manifestation produces celebration in us for them and to God while our hearts begin to wonder if maybe, just maybe, He was simply unwilling to do it for us.

If I may say it this way – there is nothing wrong with you and you are well able to produce. I will never forget the words my Husband said not too long ago, "there is nothing wrong with our reach!" What did he mean? He was speaking to our potential and our ability to produce what God had shown us. I repeat what he said in this moment, and let me say it loud so that your spirit man hears it too:

THERE IS NOTHING WRONG WITH YOUR REACH!

-Pastor Omar Rojas

There is nothing wrong with your ability! There is nothing wrong with your capacity! There is nothing wrong with your access! SPIRIT MAN WAKE UP! There is nothing wrong with your mind! There is nothing wrong with your creativity! You are not stuck – you are FREE INDEED! **SPIRIT MAN WAKE UP!** You are able to create, multiply and strive! You are able to sow and reap abundance all in the same day! Oh, yes you can! You are WELL able to do what God showed you! So what you asked for it and it did not show up for you yet, but you prayed it for someone else and it came like lightning! **YOUR PRAYERS WORK!! GOD HEARS YOU and HE IS GOING TO DO IT FOR YOU!!!**

Come through Midwife! Your time is coming! Your time is here! Your time is NOW!

What "baby" in your life needs to live? What vision are you waiting on? Write it down now!

My Life Nuggets

_____

_____

_____

_____

_____

_____

_____

_____

_____

_____

_____

_____

_____

_____

Nugget #27

Unstoppable

impossible to stop or prevent.

Here we are on nugget 27 and truthfully, by now you should feel the depth of how UNSTOPPABLE you really are! I need you to grab your superhero cape and throw that baby on because you survived it!! You are sitting in the survivor's circle and now it is time for you to thrive. There are things, thoughts and even people who have come for your life, but here you yet stand, and that deserves a celebration! No, I am not going to wait until we get to the last chapter, I am going to celebrate you right now!!!

There was a lady named Sister Jerri Pitts who attended the church I grew up in and every time she would stand to give her testimony she would always preface it by saying:

When I think of the goodness of Jesus,

And all He has done for me,

My soul cries out Hallelujah!

I thank God for saving me!

What a revelation! What a word! You see in that moment, she realized just how much God had done and how He had qualified her to be unstoppable. She would then follow it with an update of what had taken place in her life and how she was sitting in a divine place of victory. Did she face things? YES. Were there days where she did not want to even share because of what she was enduring? I know there was! The difference was this: because she had testified so many times, the people expected her to speak every time, even if it was her traditional opener. I wish you would take this next page and use it to reflect on all that God has done for you. In the face of what has tried to take you out, you still stand UNSTOPPABLE.

My Life Nuggets

_____

_____

_____

_____

_____

_____

_____

_____

_____

_____

_____

_____

_____

_____

_____

_____

Nugget #28

Oil

lubricate or coat (something) with oil.

Do you remember The Wizard of Oz, more specifically, the Tin Man? Every person in this iconic film had an issue: the lion wanted courage, the scarecrow wanted a brain, the tin man wanted a heart and Dorothy just wanted to go home! There came a point in the film where they were traveling along, all in pursuit of their desire, when the Tin Man could no longer move. The rest of the crew responded in concern, desperately trying to find out what was wrong only to find out that he could not move and could not even open his mouth to speak, all because he needed oil. He needed oil.

As vessels used for purpose and destiny, we must always keep in mind that we have to always be ready to receive fresh oil. I know, I know, you may believe that your current dispensation of "oil" is working just fine, but is it fit for where God wants to take you? I mean, can you really say that the last anointing could not be due for a fresh impartation? Sometimes, especially during altar calls, I look at the faces of those in the congregation. For the majority of that time, I am looking for those who have a desire for prayer or those who want to change their life for the best, but I also look because I can see those who need to come up if only to receive more from God, but instead they stay in their seat. Now while there are times where God will permit me to invite them up, there have also been times where I expressly felt the requirement for people to be willing to move, come and receive what they need from Him. Now do not get me wrong, God can meet us right in our seats too, but there are those moments where movement is absolutely necessary.

So let's get back to the Tin Man. There he is, standing there unable to move or speak while everyone else around him is trying to figure out what is going on with their friend. He then begins to release a sound — one that required translation in order to get what he needed, his oil can. The moment his friends realized it, they immediately went and found it and began to replenish him in the places where he was immobile. Hear me and hear me clearly — we need people in our lives who can identify when we are rusty and replenish us with the oil of God so that we all can complete the journey together! This requires vulnerability, but it also requires trust!

Who are the people in your life that can detect your deficiency and has the capacity to bring you out of your stuck places? Everyone needs at least one person who can.

My Life Nuggets

Nugget #29

Wind

*a scent carried by the wind, indicating the presence or
proximity of an animal or person.*

There was a dream I had some years ago that went
a little something like this:

I had a dream where I found myself in Florida. Now, I have
only been there a handful of times, so the fact that I was
there was surprising to me. At the time, I had a Chevrolet
HHR and my car, also known as DYmond, was in the dream
as well. A massive storm came, and I found myself running
into a building. It was gutted out, but the stained-glass
windows revealed to me that it was a church. I found a
corner to hide surrounded by the sounds of the storm and
glass shattering all around me. As quickly as the storm had
begun, it ended, and I stood up only to see that the building
was barely standing. I walked outside, but with the
exceptions of a few tree limbs, that was the only damage I
saw; even my car was still sitting upright and untouched. I

135

woke up startled and confused but eventually accepted the wave of peace that God was sending my way.

WIND — it can be considered your best friend or your worst enemy. Wind can be the worst hair stylist or the best blessing on a hot and humid day; it can be the carrier of the sand in our eyes or the push behind the pep in our step. This dream came happened before I ever became a servant leader and I truly did not receive the clarity of the dream until we began going through our own ministry storms, but those are a different caliber of stories for another day. Overall, I had to remember that the wind was how God spoke to Elijah and it was the push, along with the ocean, behind Paul making it on broken pieces in the New Testament as well. Wind, can be felt but not seen, yet we trust its presence will be there every time we inhale or exhale. It is time for you, now, to embrace the wind. It may be the thing that pushes you into a place called "uncomfortable" yet exists as the very inspiration you needed to achieve your dream. This phenomenon could be the best friend you never had that shows up if only for a moment to let you know that God really does hear your prayers.

Embrace the wind, so that you can embrace your WIN.

My Life Nuggets

_____

_____

_____

_____

_____

_____

_____

_____

_____

_____

_____

_____

_____

Nugget #30

FYre

fervent or passionate emotion or enthusiasm; luminosity; glow.

God gave me DYmondFYre while meeting with a friend one day discussing my next moves in ministry. I was nervous and did not know what I would walk away from that meeting with, but I knew that I could not leave empty-handed. We sat and tossed names around until finally we said DYmondFYre! I sat, wondering if the name was creative enough and was later assured that it was perfect. I knew that I wanted a name that described who I was once called, Diamond (later changed to DYmond), along with my igniting passion for God, FYre. Someone once asked, "why do you have your name with a "Y" instead of "IA". I could have been sassy and said it was because I felt like it but that was not the reason and even if it had been, at that stage in my life I doubt that I would have responded that way. I smiled and said:

"Because of the position of the "Y" – it's sitting in a place of worship."

139

We find countless stories in the word of God where people are faced with beyond ridiculous circumstances, only for them to break out in worship and find themselves free. Spiritual fire does not feel good, in fact, it has the propensity of hurting beyond what words can describe because of what it burns up. For one, the fire may come for relationships that are no good for the next level of our lives or maybe a mindset that we simply refuse to surrender without it being burned up. Regardless of what the FYRE comes for, please remember this:

It never burns what it does not have to ability to replace, with greater.

We just have to be honest enough to say, "God I need You to do this for me."

We have to be mature enough to say, "God if don't give this to you, I will sabotage myself."

We have to be trusting enough to know that He will take what we willingly surrender and turn it into beauty for His glory!

My Life Nuggets

_____

_____

_____

_____

_____

_____

_____

_____

_____

_____

_____

_____

_____

_____

_____

Nugget #31

Warfare

engagement in or the activities involved in war or conflict.

One of my favorite movies is called "Sucker Punch."
This story involves a girl whose stepfather allows her mother
to die in an attempt to get her inheritance. Immediately
after her death, he found her mother's will only to find out
that everything had been willed to the daughters and
nothing had been left for him. In a moment of rage, he
launched a sexual assault against the youngest daughter
and when she denied him, he killed her and blamed it on
the oldest sibling who we only know as "Babydoll"; this was
the name given to her after she was hauled off to what was
supposed to be in insane asylum but was later revealed as
a place for girls to "entertain" men. Babydoll finds herself
bonding with a few of the other girls to plan their escape,
but it does not come without WARFARE and her number one
weapon, dance.

What are your weapons of warfare?

In 2 Corinthians 10:4-5 we find these words:

"⁴ The weapons of our warfare are not physical [weapons of flesh and blood]. Our weapons are divinely powerful for the destruction of fortresses. ⁵ We are destroying sophisticated arguments and every exalted *and* proud thing that sets itself up against the [true] knowledge of God, and *we are* taking every thought *and* purpose captive to the obedience of Christ."

Battles won do not come absent of warfare. I cannot tell you how many times I have expressed that I was tired of fighting but felt the bigger One on the inside of me demanding me to continue pushing. One of the main things we have to remember is that the warfare knows that it has no right to overtake us, but we have to know it, and that is when it counts! The warfare that shows up for us cannot be fought or overcome with carnal weapons, in other words, our "world" resolves will not work, but instead we must tap into the spiritual authority we have been given from the very start to go from victim to victor! You can do this, no matter what the circumstance!

Are you ready?

FIGHT – and WIN.

My Life Nuggets

Nugget #32

Rest

cease work or movement in order to relax, refresh oneself, or recover strength;

allow to be inactive in order to regain strength, health, or energy.

Now this one has been one of the hardest areas for me to master, and to be honest, I am still learning to do so. I often say that out of everything I was taught during the process of licensing, ordination and serving, one of the things they never taught us was the importance or process of REST. For visionaries, this oftentimes proves to be a hard place of conversation, especially since we are always moving and often working even in our sleep.

Recently, an area pastor announced to his congregation that after eleven years of preaching and 5,000 sermons later, he needed a sabbatical. (For those that may not know, sabbatical is a fancy way of saying "REST.) With tears in his eyes, he expressed that he was not going anywhere but simply needed a time to reset himself, because he now saw and felt just how out of touch with God he was. He said, "I want to know what this phenomenon called "brunch' is." See, while many people's worship time is limited to the time they spend in the house of God and the impartation they receive, the one that will not rest finds themselves still at church even when they are not there, or even being physically there while their "mind is on the other side of town."

When we take time to rest, it is literally a restorative act; not only does it replenish our cells, but it also makes us more equipped to handle the day's event successfully. When we rest, we are able to think more clearly, are less irritable and more productive. I was doing it wrong before so please do not be like pre-me: I thought that as long as I was always moving and grinding with my three hours of sleep, I would be ok, but not so. Now I know that I have to take time for me and that I am no good to anyone if I am unable to function. (You may feel like I should have 'just known that,' but in all honestly I ignored it because of what I felt like I just had to do.)

Rest baby rest. God's got you!

My Life Nuggets

Nugget #33

Silence

the state of standing still and not speaking as a sign of respect for someone deceased or in an opportunity for prayer.

Have you ever been in time out? Now, my mom will probably get me for this one, so please do not tell her that I told you, but I was too scared to act up in school, so the most I ever had was afterschool detention and I was in tenth grade then. We sat in the cafeteria at separate tables and yes, literally, just sat there. I felt like I was part of that movie, The Breakfast Club, minus the fun!

Throughout the word of God, there are occurrences where God does not speak for years, and I mean seventy years or even four hundred years; He literally responded in SILENCE. I know how the conversations go, my conversations anyway, when I feel like God has me in time out. Take the last quarter of 2019 for instance: how does God put you in time out so much so, that He even deters you from the platforms where you felt most comfortable. Now let's be real shall we, it was not until God took me through this that I realized that I had a major problem not going live or sharing and simply allowing God to pour without me breaking my silence. Remember I told you earlier that I was the kid that wanted to share everything and God's refueling for me was no different. This time though, He required my silence. There were days that I had major things to share but He would not even allow my fingers to compose the words. Every part of me wanted to say something but God would not allow it — His silence became my silence and I had to respect it.

The next level of silence I experienced was through worship. I would give my all as always and leave feeling depleted and feeling nothing. I could not understand and became afraid, feeling that maybe God had disconnected from me only to realize that He had no reply because He was calling me higher and the currently level of worship was no longer suitable for the next dimension that He required of me. So yes, I had to go higher and continue to do so because it is what God requires of me.

You may be afraid of heights, but higher is calling. Come out of time out.

My Life Nuggets

Nugget #34

Strategy

a plan of action or policy designed to achieve a major or overall aim.

As we personally sit on the brink of a new year, many people are sitting and writing goals and that is wonderful but are also forsaking STRATEGY! There is nothing wrong with seeing the vision but there must be a set of instructions on how you will get there. As you continue to read, I pray that this blesses you and causes you to begin writing on the next page.

You will never see a contractor head out, clear land randomly and start throwing down concrete and throwing up sticks! Why? Because they understand that the building has the capacity to be deemed unsafe and hurt countless people if he does not have a plan, a blueprint, that he can follow. This is where the architect comes in — the one who brings the vision to life. They create the plan and present the manifestation of the visionary. If you are anything like me, you are self-motivated. In other words, if I do not know how to do it, I will do my best to figure it out or position myself to learn it! This has caused me to always remain to be a student, as there are things God has called me to do without a physical teacher but has also sent people along the way to help and mentor me along.

In this year, I want to encourage you to be willing to not just stop at the vision and take off running, but to also take the time needed to develop the STRATEGY so that you can have what you saw. If this means that you have to bring in a demolition crew, do it! God would rather build you back up right, instead of trying to build you on shaky and unstable ground.

Let this be your prayer:

Lord, I need You to make me over again. I give you all I have and all I have done and tried to do for your glory. I did not do it all right, but I pray for your grace, mercy and wisdom as I press forward to build RIGHT! Thank you Father for another chance – this time, it is going to work!

AMEN.

My Life Nuggets

Nugget #35

Mentor

advise or train (someone, especially a younger colleague).

Mentorship is something I hold near and dear to my heart. I can truly say that I have been blessed with some of the best mentors and that they all, both past and present, have imparted something in my life that I use even until this day. It is so very important to have a mentor – someone who can, as my husband Pastor Omar Rojas often says, "see further than you can look." We need people in our lives who can celebrate us when we are right and get us right when we are wrong without our attitude being the response. As a mentor, I have had those who have taken my words and ran with them and others who heard the words I knew God gave me for them, got upset and disappeared, but as a mentor God often entrusts us with the hard word!

One of my most impactful mentors was an amazing Woman of God named Sheonette Brown, who passed away over five years ago. During one of the worst places of my life, she invited me to come to the church and help her on the administration end. I was not sure why she invited me, but for me it was definitely an opportunity to get out of the house and get what was happening off of my mind. There we sat day after day, answering phones and stuffing envelopes, while she shared nuggets with me along the way and gave me "breaks" by sending me to the post office to drop off the church's outgoing mail. (I now believe that was her way of giving me some time to process the bombs she dropped on me!) Prior to her death, I was in a really bad place – I was in ministry, serving as pastor and just coming into the revelation of some of the things that had been around me all my life; it literally felt like God was taking away my entire childhood as I was faced with abandonment from those I shared countless memories with. I called in tears, not knowing the severity of her condition, which she kept hidden very well. As I expressed my heartache she said:

"Do I need to get out of my bed and come to your house?"

My reply was faint but sure, as I sniffled, "no ma'am," into the phone. She then said these words:

"Woman of God! Woman of Zion! Mother of Zion!

Get up, wipe off your face! Keep going!"

I recovered quickly in that moment, hearing the fire in her voice and the demand in her words. This conversation served as the last one we had prior to her death on November 28, 2019 but these words have stuck with me and carried me through so many places that she never had the opportunity to see.

A mentor should always leave a word with you that will live far beyond their presence in your life.

My Life Nuggets

_____

_____

_____

_____

_____

_____

_____

_____

_____

_____

_____

_____

_____

_____

Nugget #36

Balance

stability of one's mind or feelings; an even distribution of weight enabling someone or something to remain upright and steady.

Oh, the roles we play and the hats we wear!

Husband and Wife

Mother and Father

Sister and Brother

Friend and Confidant

Associate and Affiliation

Visionary and Innovator

This list does not even probably begin touch the brink of all you do but serves as a starting place! BALANCE, this place of even weight everywhere, seems crazy and maybe even impossible, but can exist when we demand it. When I first became a servant leader, I bombarded my time being just that, a servant leader. I say

163

this with the deepest humility, I found myself being a servant leader so much that I gave "crumbs" to everything else. In our minds, those around us should just understand, right? Well, what about those moments when they need us and receive our attitudes or neglect in response? They do not deserve it, but it becomes our deepest hope that they will just – understand.

If you do not activate anything else in this moment, accept the fact that it is okay to have balance. People will always have their demands, but their demands cannot engulf the beauty of the balance required for your life. Now am I saying there will never be sacrifices? Absolutely not! There will times where those on the outside will look at you in sheer confusion because of the balancing act you are in, nevertheless, it is required for the end goal. No worries, God will show you what is what, and when it is time for you to re-calibrate He will let you know that, too.

As you sit in this moment, ask yourself the following:

Am I balanced or out of balance?

What can I do to re-calibrate myself?

What are some things that I need to activate in my life for the sake of my own balance?

My Life Nuggets

Nugget #37

Grace

simple elegance or refinement of movement;

Maybe I should adopt this saying:

You don't look like what you have been through!

You, yes you, do not even begin to look like what you have been through or endured and a huge part of that is because of God's grace extended to all of us. Grace, I promise you, is so underserved. I can look back over my life and know that if my faults had been subject to man, I would have been outcasted by now, but God's grace on my life did not allow it. That being said, let's talk about grace extended to others.

People are not perfect (no not even you.) We are vessels subject to faults and making mistakes. Sometimes, the grace we extend is conditional – we give it to one but retract it from another. We may even be guilty of holding grace because it has happened too many times, so now someone has to be made an example of. Know this – it is

167

hard to receive God's grace, if we refuse to extend grace to those who need it. Our debts oftentimes have what is called a grace-period, and some of us have even had grace on the grace period. Am I advising that you be foolish? No, but I am advising that you know the difference. There are people that have paid high costs, all because the deserved grace but could not receive It because the source they needed it from was bleeding out. Many become critical of people who do things they have never, ever done, all because they do not know how to extend grace but have become a perfectionist at being critical and overbearing.

Who has suffered all because you refuse to extend GRACE?

My Life Nuggets

_____

_____

_____

_____

_____

_____

_____

_____

_____

_____

_____

_____

_____

_____

_____

Nugget #38

Favor

approval, support, or liking for someone or something; overgenerous preferential treatment.

Have you ever been in a drive-thru line and had someone you do not know pay for your food? Have you ever been in a restaurant and had someone you do not know pay for your food at the very moment you needed it? Been there, done that and the feeling is indescribable.

One day, my lead armor bearer and a fellow member of our congregation were coming from a mountain retreat. We were already on cloud nine as we considered all God had done and on the way decided to stop for an early dinner. As we parked, I did not tell them, but I began counting my money in my head; I knew exactly how much I had, and though it was my last, I wanted to sow it there with them. As we walked in, it felt like the whole room was staring at us (or it could have been us because that weekend was like WHOA!) As we sat, I remember saying:

"I wonder who is going to pay for our meal today! Do it God!"

We ordered and we ate. I sat and subconsciously waited for someone to say, "it's already covered," but then the bill showed up. I nodded my head, acknowledging the tab, and said, "Ok, well I guess it's gonna happen next time." I pulled out the money I had, and my armor bearer went to pay the bill. The next thing I knew, she came rushing around the corner and said:

"PASTOR! THERE IS NO BILL!"

Now in my head I was looking like a Spike Lee movie with the background moving, but staying as cool as I could I said, "Repeat that!" As she said it again, I smiled and thanked God because I knew that His FAVOR showed up that day. There was nothing I did to deserve it, but because He is my Father, He made it happen for us that day!

I need you to receive the favor of God now.

Allow any pride to fall away and simply remain postured to receive.

FAVOR IS COMING FOR YOU!

My Life Nuggets

Nugget #39

Power

*the ability to do something or act in a particular way,
especially as a faculty or quality;*

*the capacity or ability to direct or influence the behavior of
others or the course of events.*

I recently taught a series called DOMINATE and boy
was it a doozy! In it, we discovered the pitfalls and
successes of manifested domination in every area of our
lives. We talked about the things that were holding us back
and the things we needed to activate in order to dominate.
Here is the scripture that we used:

**Listen carefully: I have given you authority [that you now
possess] to tread on [a]serpents and scorpions, and [the
ability to exercise authority] over all the power of the
enemy (Satan); and nothing will [in any way] harm you.**

Luke 10:19

Here we are – POWER!! We have been given
POWER to tread over serpents and scorpions and POWER

175

to exercise authority over the enemy too! We have been given POWER to walk in our God-given authority and we SHOULD, but first we have to be sure that our POWER is turned ON! Hold up, wait a minute, turned ON? Yes, TURNED ON! Power does not work unless it is turned on! Are your breakers on? Is your switch on? Are you really ready for the POWER that is waiting for your arrival? When God comes to deliver power unto you, where will He find you? When your dream needs a power source, will it be able to get it from you? There are possessions waiting! Joy is waiting! Peace is waiting for you! Are you willing to wait for power? I am telling you, and this is coming from someone who has had their power turned off, when you are powerless you never forget that feeling and never want to feel it again, so you give it your all just to make sure that you always have it.

Powerless moments show up, but it does not mean that you cannot become POWERFUL. There is a word in your DNA that can only be activated by you and I tapping into POWER.

The thing that feels like it is still waiting – may just be waiting for your POWER to turn on, so that it knows it is free to show up!

POWER is here. Grab it, hold tight and do not let go! You are worth every ounce of POWER God has invested in you!

My Life Nuggets

_____

_____

_____

_____

_____

_____

_____

_____

_____

_____

_____

_____

_____

_____

Nugget #40

Growth

the process of developing or maturing physically, mentally, or spiritually.

I do not have a "green thumb" but I do have the capacity to help things grow. I have spent years digging up ground, putting down fertilizer and helping other plants grow. When it outgrew the space it was in, I would help it go to a bigger place. Here is the problem – I did not think that I deserved to grow like that but only felt I could help others get to that place. Every time I began to know the truth, BOOM, something would happen to knock me down! The more I realized the bloodline resting in me, the more things came against me in an attempt to take my confidence and my drive. I simply did not believe that what I helped others do ever deserved to be me, but TODAY.

I modeled for years and trust, this profession comes with a look of confidence that others may fully believe but may not even be present. I once went from modeling to teaching others to do the same – I had my walk down and would teach them the ropes for the upcoming shows. My confidence was low, but I had a gift of helping others feel, look and walk like billionaires. Oh, the feeling of being on that stage and seeing others do the same, only to say in my head that they do it better than me, even when I taught them.

God, thank You for GROWTH. It took me 40 years to finally say that I deserve it, too! What is IT?

Success, Freedom, Life, Confidence, Overflow!

I deserve it too and so do you! If you have settled for the crumbs of life, it is now time for you to demand the whole loaf. This may mean getting in crowds where no one knows who you are! Maybe it means doing something that you have never done or never imagined you would do. For you, it may be going back to school, yes to complete what you started! WHEW! Whatever GROWTH looks like, I need you to embrace it. God needs you to prepare for it.

It's time to reverse the sabotage and walk in FULL PURPOSE!

My Life Nuggets

_____

_____

_____

_____

_____

_____

_____

_____

_____

_____

_____

_____

_____

Nugget #41

Identity

the fact of being who or what a person or thing is.

God has called me to be amazing.

He has called me to be kind.

He has ordained me to be a vessel that He can use.

He is the catapult of my destiny.

He has crafted me by design.

I recently saw a documentary that said that the personality and characteristics of a baby are developed in the womb starting from that point of the mother being approximately sixteen weeks pregnant. Our DNA, already at work, begins to develop our skin tone, eye color, hair texture and the whole nine yards. Our fingers and toes are developed with distinct fingerprints included. We come forth in IDENTITY that we not even come to the knowledge of yet.

Sometimes, I wonder why the enemy has come for me so much and only one answer makes sense, my IDENTITY!

This word includes so much, as it entails everything about us that someone would need to know in order to properly identify who we are in the earth and in the spirit. You may be that person that looks at your life and says, "it's not that big of a deal; I am just doing what I do," but baby, your IDENTITY is doing more than you can possibly imagine. In the beginning, The Word came forth saying:

26 Then God said, "Let Us (Father, Son, Holy Spirit) make man in Our image, according to Our likeness [not physical, but a spiritual personality and moral likeness]; and let them have complete authority over the fish of the sea, the birds of the air, the cattle, and over the entire earth, and over everything that creeps *and* crawls on the earth."

Genesis 1:26

From the very start you were a force to be reckoned with! Filled with power, ability and authority, God created a reflection of Him that would make Satan fall to his knees. He set a fire in your soul that has the capacity to destroy the most well-thought out plan against your life. He arrested your vocal cords and called forth a sound that make the gates of hell fall at your feet and make every plot of wickedness give up the ghost! You, yes you! Please know that in this moment, God is equipping you and activating you! He is stirring you up and preparing you for the greatest days and decades of your life! He is bringing you forth as a generational curse breaker and a blessing activator!

He is dusting off your grave clothes and bringing you into another realm of GLORY, yes RIGHT NOW! He is re-focusing you and bringing you into this, the decade of the mouth! In this moment, you have the invitation and option to have what He spoke! Are you ready? Are you set? GOOD.

I will SEE it! I will SAY it! I will HAVE IT. Let's go get it!

AMEN AND AMEN!

My Life Nuggets

_____

_____

_____

_____

_____

_____

_____

_____

_____

_____

_____

_____

_____

_____

_____

Connect with the Author

Brandi L. Rojas

Wife | Mother | Pastor | Author | Mentor | Entrepreneur | Visionary Author

Pastor Brandi L. Rojas is a native and resident of Greensboro, N.C. She serves with her Husband, Pastor Omar Rojas at Maximizing Life Family Worship Center in Greensboro, N.C., a vision God birthed through them in 2015. Rojas has been in Dance Ministry for over 20 years and is a 2009 graduate of the School of Disciples taught under the late Bishop Otis Lockett, Sr. Pastor Rojas was licensed to preach the Gospel on February 27, 2011 in Thomasville, N.C., and as a result DYmondFYre Global Ministries was born. Rojas was ordained as an Ordained Elder June 2012, was installed as Pastor with her Husband, Pastor Omar Rojas in January 2013 and now serves as Executive Pastor for the vision God has assigned to them through #MaxLife.

Since that time, she and her Husband, also known as #TeamRojas, by God's mandate, have been honored in the marketplace and birthed several evangelistic causes. In 2013, Rojas was named Sweetheart of the Triad, an award

187

given based on community involvement. In January 2014, Rojas opened FYreDance Studios and Liturgical Arts Consulting which provides on-site instruction, virtual teaching, consultation services, choreography services and deliverance and healing dance encounters. In that same year, after serving with Pastor Cassandra Elliott and The Gathering Experience for two years, she began serving and currently serves as the Lead Dance Vessel Coordinator for this time of worship amongst those who are hungry, thirsty and desperate for the presence of God. The following year a prayer walk initiative was created to bring the local churches and community together to work together and help lead the lost to Jesus Christ and empower the world through a vehicle called The Gatekeeper's Legacy; she has also served as part of the planning and leadership committee for the National Day of Prayer for the City of Greensboro and currently serves as the youngest committee member, only African-American and only female on the core team.

In February 2016, Rojas launched out again to begin The Legacy Ladies Fellowship, an organization created to help women of God pray, push and live the reality of what God has called them to do. Most recently to this list of mandates, The CrossOver Resource Center was added, working to provide solutions for life's transitions to the community. Rojas released her first book in June 2016 entitled <u>In the Face of Expected Failure</u> and her sophomore project, <u>Humpty Dumpty in Stilettos: The Great Exchange</u>, in November 2016. It was with the second book release Fiery Beacon Publishing House was launched, serving current and upcoming authors, playwrights, poets, blog writers and more. <u>Humpty Dumpty in Stilettos</u> was nominated for the national Literary Trailblazer of the Year Award in June 2017 by the Indie Author Legacy Award in Baltimore, Maryland and in July 2017 she was noted as an International Best-Selling Author for her part in a collaborative effort called <u>Stories from the Pink Pulpit: Women in Ministry Speak</u>. Rojas is also a two-time nominee for Trailblazer of the Year, Choreographer of the Year and Women of Inspiration with ACHI Women Supporting Women, Inc. She is currently preparing for her next solo release, <u>Rehobeth Church Road: Suicide in the Pulpit</u> and is celebrating the first publishing company collaboration for Fiery Beacon Publishing House entitled, <u>When Legacy Arises from the Threshing Floor: A Collective of Trials and Tribulations Superseded by Undeniable Triumphs!</u>

In the Marketplace, Pastor Rojas is also known for her progressive efforts through her travel company, DYmondFYre Destinations and the international platform of Surge365 where she makes it a priority to share the reality and necessity of multiple streams of income which empowers the home, community, nation and world. Pastor Rojas is grateful and humbled at how God continues to expand the entire vision, not just to the United States, but internationally as well.

#Team Rojas are the proud parents of five children. Pastor Brandi Rojas is a Worshiper, Servant, Praise Vessel, and Prayer Warrior, but most of all, she is a vessel who is on fire for God.

Wife I Mother I Pastor I Author I Mentor I Entrepreneur I Visionary

https://www.linktr.ee/dymondfyre

https://www.linktr.ee/fierybeaconpublishinghousellc

IG and Twitter: @allthingsdymondfyre and @maxlifedfg

Fiery Beacon
PUBLISHING HOUSE

Greensboro, North Carolina

Phone: (336) 285-5794

fierybeaconcpg@gmail.com

Get your other Fiery Beacon favorites by

Pastor Brandi Rojas today!

In the Face of Expected Failure

Humpty Dumpty in Stilettos: The Great Exchange

When Legacy Arises from the Threshing Floor:

Trials and Tribulations Superseded by Undeniable Victories

Stories from the Pink Pulpit: Women in Ministry Speak

(Collaboration by Dr. Marilyn E. Porter)

Rehobeth Church Road: Suicide in the Pulpit

When Legacy Arises from the Threshing Floor: Volume 2

Before You Hit 40: Forty-One Pivotal Life Nuggets

Not With Your Legs Crossed: #SpiritualBirthingUncensored

My Pink Stilettos

The Mantle I Never Asked For

Talitha Koum: Get Up Little Girl, GET UP!

Build It A-GAIN: Confessions of the Nehemiah Generation